Journey to Love

40 Letters Dedicated to Love
Vol. 1

By: Booker Snow

Zeroed Out Publishing

Zeroed Out Publishing book may be purchased for
educational, business, or sales promotional use.

FIRST EDITION
Designed by A. Washington

Type of Work: Text
Registration Number / Date: TXu002184137 / 2020-02-06
Title: Journey to Love 40 Letters Dedicated to Love Vol. 1.
Copyright Claimant: Booker B Snow III
Date of Creation: 2019
Authorship on Application: Booker Bernard Snow III;
Citizenship: United States.
Authorship: text.
Rights and Permissions: Booker Snow
Copyright Note: Basis for Registration: Collective work.
Names: Snow, Booker Bernard, III
Snow, Booker B, III

Cover design and image by A. Washington. Cover images
© 2019 by Zeroed Out Publishing. Editor Chey DLC.
Foreword by Kahina Astraea Vashti Aphrodite. Biography
and back of book by JoAnna Menzie. Photograph by Mark
Jordan for Orange County Headshots.

Foreword

Poet Booker Snow III welcomes you along for the ride as
he travels to, through and with Love. Along his journey,
he manifests words into morsels for ingestion and
expresses rich and varied textures to be felt; tastes to be
savored; emotions to be reveled in. Booker writes with
every color creating a portrait of Love and its multi-
faceted contradictions. With honest vulnerability, he
paints in words that ignite the cherished recollection of a
love brand new, brimming with promise, and dreams of a
love not yet realized but anticipated. Booker's writing
inspires one to savor each syllable and if you find yourself
whispering his prose aloud,
- allow the words to float from your lips into a prayer of
gratitude, or a prayer of want, as a wish or as a promise
and bask in both the possibility and the reality of Love.
Love is messy
Love is perplexing.
Love is blinding insightful clarity,
Love makes sense of the mess and love gets you all the
way together.
Love takes shape in fleeting and repeating sparks of light
Love suddenly overwhelms with waves of torrential force.
Love's potential burdens with awkward insecurity
Love infuses a confidence never known
without warning you're flying – weightless
Love is chemical reactions
Love is a Spiritual connection.

Love is unexpected familiarity wrapped in the yet-to-be-
discovered,
their greatest regret
her favorite color
the origin of his scars.
Love makes you want more.
Love makes you want nothing else
Love increases your heart rate and your breathing while
simultaneously freezing time.
Love is everlasting
Love is temporary
Love is both
Love is an open road stretching beyond present
perception, no way of knowing if it culminates in a hidden
cliff.
- still, each step forward, taken in bliss.
Love is Faith over fear.

-Kahina Astraea Vashti Aphrodite

If I never have another night to live
If I never have another breath to give
If I never get to see another day
I can't allow this moment to get away.
I've made a lot of tough decisions
Good intentions guided all my years
Most of which all left me broken
I closed my eyes to hold in the tears.
As I walk the remainder of my journey
I know its best that you're told
I've always wanted to know you.
To Love you. To see where it all goes.
I might be late in my admission
But I hope my submission is clear
I'm sorry it took me so long...
To get past my hurt, my thoughts, my fear.
Please excuse my selfishness
I apologize for my words of disruption
I know this may be a bit to take in
But I beg you, pardon my interruption.
You're the one that I wanted to learn
You're the one that I wanted to adore
You're the one that I wanted to admire
You're the one that I wanted to support.
I wanted to be the comfort amidst cries
I wanted to be the relax at stressful times.
I wanted to be peace that piece your heart
The anything you needed for us not to be apart...

Your intelligence. Your beauty. Your beliefs. Your time.
Your everything is amazing I wish it was mine...

From a seed planted years ago, yesterday I watched a life
bloom.
The atmosphere was created for this process to resume.
The soil was fertile and perfectly tilled.
There was a perfect light covering the field.
Information flowed like a stream to hydrate the seed.
As specific conversation fulfilled the rest of its needs.
The earth moved gently.
Time stood still.
This is unreal, as the first leaf made its reveal.

... It was beautiful.

You're so close right now
It's not the distance, it's the feel.
You're so close right now
Day to day life has become more real.
Every moment is more precious.
You're a fine detail.
An amazing mood.
An attitude to exhibit.
The definition in the room.
You're so close right now
I'm excited and can barely stay still.
You're so close right now
I understand why my broken heart had to heal.
You're so close right now
I can finally ask...
"Excuse me. May I have please this dance?"
Every day can be OUR prom.
Endless days of romance if given the chance.
All because, you're so close right now.

Whenever you're ready. Whenever you've decided.
Whenever you're tired. Remember, you've been invited.
Whatever you propose. Whatever you engage.
Whatever dates you chose I'm here all the same.
If you stay or go. If you have it or don't.
If you know or not. I'm all good with the flow.
Wherever you are. Wherever you land.
Wherever you live it's cool, I'm your man.

Allow me to elaborate...

When you're ready to choose, I've already decided I'm
going to love you. So when you're tired and don't want to
be alone. Remember, you've been invited. The door's
open and, here's THE key. I'll always be your home.

Our lives will never be the same. Lord willing, I'm here. So
it's whatever time you choose. I'm ready to date as long
as I get to spend those moments with you.

I'm down for whatever we propose, at least until I
eventually take a knee. I'll always lovingly engage you.
Support you. Need you. Want you. Fuck the talk, I'll show
and prove you so you can see.

If you stay, I'll stay. If you go, I'll go. I want to be a team
and every great leader knows when to lead and when to
follow.

If you have it, bet! I'll have it to match. If we don't have it, we'll get it! Let's develop a plan of attack. If you know already, I'm listening full attention. If you don't have a clue, it's cool let's stop and think for a minute.

You feel that? It's an all-natural organic flow....

So, IF you stay where you are. I promise, give me time and I will come and meet you. Wherever you decide to go. If you're there, so is hope. I promise to come and see you.

If you have the energy or if you don't. Love, listen... you can have mine. We can share it and let it reciprocate it until the end of time.

Fill each other up with knowledge, wisdom and understanding. Love is easy and willing, not hard and demanding.

You get it yet? Do you agree or disagree with what was just said? Good. Because either way it goes, I know that I'm your man.

I'll listen. I'll hear you. I'll pay close attention.
Give me all your anguish. I'll absorb the remission.

Lean on me. I'll reduce the pressure. Fall into my arms.
Servicing you is my pleasure. When exhaustion hits. Don't
deal with it on your own. We're both strong individually,
but together we will help each other move on.

Love, I'm fully engulfed. Let me submerge. When you
speak I listen deep to your every word.
I enjoy taking you all in. All! Not some. I want to discover
you each day. Explore your every need and want.

As I listen, I'll hear you. I'll never stop paying close
attention. Speak your Love languages through the
anguish. I'm ready Love. With zero fear. Until time is
finished.

For this long-awaited re-acquaintance.
I'd rather die in my attempts than not trying to make it.
Every risk in the world, I'm willing to take it.
I've waited too long... crazy thing is I'm still being patient.
No danger exists. No warning provided.
Can keep me from this much needed alliance.
I've dreamt of your hands calmingly caressing my face.
The anxiousness of being able to wrap my arms around your waist.
Evaluating you and moving that one piece of hair to behind your ear.
Saying "hello" as our eyes lock for the first time in about 20 years.
Can we have a conversation in a diner?
Can we discuss various points of views?
Can I tell you I Love your thoughts...?
Your atmosphere, your heart, aptitude?
I'm not in a rush.
Although, I'd be lying to say I'm not anxious.
I want to meet you again for the first time.
But, in the meantime I'm waiting.
No one else can have my eye.
No one else can have my moments.
No one else can have...me.
Because of my drive, hope and focus. On you.

I can't stop smiling. How about you?

I can't stop thinking that every Love song is somehow about you.

Like you're the one that inspired every lyric, every procession, every drum.

The long-standing effect of horns and keys.

The aftermath of vocals that could make a tear run.

Your voice is like a lullaby that I have to hear to rest.

You're that sound that reminds me "young man, you're blessed."

Words of inspiration.

Stories of war, pain and triumph intrigue me.

Your philosophies and morality.

You're a beautiful human being.

You have me constantly walking to a rhythm that keeps life on beat.

I can only hope I give that feeling back.

If it's anything like your track, mine sounds sweet!!!

Tell me whatever crosses your mind & heart because it's a beautiful tune.

Thanks to you, I can now put a name and face to my mood.

I had a little down time and since you're constantly on my mind I decided reach out to say Hi.

No questions. No favors. Nothing deep. Nothing major. I just felt the need to hit you up.

Hopefully I'm not the contact that makes you say, "man, what does this dude want!?"

Well, my time has drawn nigh, but while the moment was tranquil. Hi.

I appreciate you. Enjoy your day. Thank you.

The moon shimmering off the water making a trail to take.
The sun peeking through autumn leaves as a gentles breeze blows from heaven's sake.
The heat that's just hot enough to produce sweat on your brow.
The cool outdoors gives balance. It's cold for a reason.
I didn't understand, at least until now.
Today I heard the wind & trees sing as nature's creatures completed the serenade.
I never heard such a beautiful sound.
I drift away as the music play.
I didn't know I was surrounded by so much beauty.
I never embraced it fully.
Until I woke up today. To a message.
The allure alone was enough to lure me.

I know we'll be the best this is easy to profess.
I promise we'll say the most whenever we say less. Your
presence is the essence of a Love that I confess. You're
the answer to my prayers. Dear Love, I know I'm blessed.
Stress won't be an issue. I'm always chill and loyal.
Humbled to be yours. Every day I get to know you.
Earn your trust daily. It's essential that we last.
Been wanting you forever. Now forever is the task.
I don't require much. Hear your voice. Feel your touch.
Whisper things in your ear with hopes to make you blush.
Ain't no other woman. You're the only I want.
You beautiful. You sexy but this ain't about lust.
No rush. No fuss. You the baddest. Ice cold.
Just know, you fantastic. High class. So amazing.
Excellent. You're perfect in my eyes, Love I know your
heaven sent.

You are...
Everything beautiful.
These aren't just words.
You're everything beautiful.
Whatever beautiful occurs.
The sunset, the sunrise Autumn and Spring.
You're everything beautiful.
Whatever beautiful brings.
You're everything beautiful.
Bright sun, full moon.
You're everything beautiful.
Happy times, good news.
You're everything beautiful.
That one perfect dress.
A night walk holding hands.
Knowing every moment is blessed.
You are...

Dear Love,

The clock's ticking and I believe it's our time. Yeah, we might receive some objections, people pissed because none of them were either of our selections. They'll be fine. Honestly, I don't care about their perceptions. As long as we're cool and we make our connections. On everything, Love you've got my full attention. The crazy thing is, I'm all yours in my heart, body, soul & mind. Everything is literally based on God's plan and a specific amount of time passing by.

Sincerely, Peace.

Love will be mine.
Love will be adored.
Love will be patient.
Love will mature.
Love will be valued.
Love will never decrease.
Love will never look backwards.
Love will meet Peace.

Every day we get closer and I'm so fascinated by every piece of your being.
Your blessings. Your experiences. Your thoughts.
Your feelings.
Your hustle. Your words. Your history. Your now.
Your later.
There's no way I would have ever guessed that I'd actually have a chance to be with the woman of my dreams.
You're not some romanticized image that I lust for.
You are (Love) and I can't wait to tell you that I'm in love with you.
In due time.
Until then, I want to become your friend.
Your confidant. Your lover. Your man.

Will haters call us ambitious?
Will jealousy call us foolish?
Is it the envy in their hearts?
That make em wish that they could do it?
Do we really even care?
We won't quit from what we're doing
Every day I want to learn you
So I'll never stop pursuing.
I might repeat some questions
Instead of frontin like I knew it.
If there's something to take over
I know that we can rule it.
Side by side. Building legacy
Neither of us complacent
I love when you disagree
Cause there's knowledge that I'm takin.
If we're ever separated
Na Love I'm waitin.
I know my realization
Accepting my destination....

I want you, how you want to be wanted.
Not to be simply paraded and flaunted.
But celebrated and appreciated consistently and often.
Cherish and honor you.
Check my personal ambitions.
Learn to match our frequencies instead working off
intentions.

I'm looking to grant wishes, fantasies and dreams.
 Not arguments and wasted moments, apology trinkets
and things.
I'd rather it be kind words, actions, Love hugs and kisses.
To be your fire and desire, to admire your intuition.
See, if there's hardship and we have opposite opinions.
We can converse and accept there will always be
differences.

...and that's a good thing. Love, be my all.

You are, you are, you are, you are... Life.
You are, you are, you are, you are... Hope.
You are, you are, you are, you are... Kindness.
You are, you are, you are, you are... Love.
You are, you are, you are, you are... Dreams.
You are, you are, you are, you are... Inspiration.
You are, you are, you are, you are... Comfort.
You are, you are, you are, you are... Restoration.

My forever blooming flower.
My fine detailed design.
Wonderfully crafted by the Creator.
By a God truly divine.
Footprints in the sand for me to follow written in braille.
I'd be foolish not to approach, study and shadow this trail.
I'm not one for hidden messages, agendas or squandered intervals.
I'd rather be unambiguous, transparent and keep the nonsense minimal.
Suppose you can convey the full array of your poetic prose.
Allow me to ingest your dialect and inspect the scent of your blue rose.

Dear Love,

I'm writing you this with hope that it finds you and assist you in finding me. I'll pour out my soul to give you whatever information you seek.

Whatever is essential for you to know, I'm open to enlighten. I want to give you the necessary knowledge needed to hopefully keep you excited.

Excited about our first actual introduction. I mean, we're the same but we aren't. No blinders, no assumptions, no disruptions to set us apart.

You're YOU and I'm me. We come together to forge a collaboration of Love and Peace.

I can talk about how beautiful you are all day long.
I can easily recite reflections of perceptions from
thousands of songs.
For you, it's not that hard to go far into storylines and
poems.
I can go through years of life scenarios to say how I found
Love beyond the harm.

As your voice alludes a steady flow of kinetic energy.
My heart begins to beat rapidly.
Mood reacts happily.
Perhaps this could be prosperity as we converse
intellectually.
Discussing business, emotions, travel and overcoming
tragedy.
The mind may retrospect but the existing interjects.
As discussions of progression takes relevance in dialect.
There is no perfect flow to our engagements, but I Love it.
Whatever happens next as long as you're there...I want it.

Hi, are you alone?
Will you have a moment to be free?
If so, can I call sometime today?
I just want you to be secure with me.
Please tell me about your day.
Is everything with you okay?
I know we're far away.
But you're with me every step of the way.
Love, I hope you feel the same.
I'd be lying to say that this is easy.
I want eternity in your arms.
I'm hoping that you will need me.
I want to be wherever you are.
To study and learn all of your ways.
To understand all of your habits.
To tell you I love you every day.

Dreams of your happiness
Written stories in the stars
Rain drops dance melodically
Distance doesn't make you far.
Heavenly designed
Lines drawn in hand conjoin
Forge eventual memories
Present futures enjoyed.
A whisper in the wind
A diamond in the dark
A candle in a window
The time healed heart.
Lightning strikes sand
Adoration desires
Pulsate rhythmic heat
Your love to be acquired.

Going out to enjoy yourself?
I'll be here when you return.
To remind you we are a home
A legacy. A Love. A forge.
Don't ever feel forced to choose.
You can go. You can stay.
Please, enjoy the abundance of life Just come back to me safe.
If you ever feel the need to play
Or walk through nature's bliss,
Go, speak privately to God
But while gone, you will be missed.
Travel and continue to discover
Your voyages are far from complete.
Sometimes I will join you,
Sometimes I'll watch you leave.
Going out to enjoy yourself?
I'll be here when you return.
To remind you we are a home
A legacy. A Love. A forge.
Don't ever feel forced to choose.
You can go. You can stay.
Please, enjoy the abundance of life Just come back to me safe.
You don't have to feel conflicted.
There's no need to feel concerned.
My peace is with you always
My loyalty can't be tested or turned.

So go. Have worriless fun. Enjoy.
Frolic in God's splendor.
Just know your welcome back will be great
Whether it was days, hours, seconds, or minutes.

Good morning cotton candy cloud covered sky.
Good morning brisk breeze whisking by.
Good morning multicolored fall leaves.
Good morning Father meeting all our needs.
Good morning children parading to the bus.
Good morning butterfly as gentle wings touch.
Good morning squirrels enjoying a morning play.
Good morning dawn starting another day
Good morning graceful small water stream.
Good morning sunshine daylight beam.
Good morning all-natural scents.
Good morning life we appreciate this.
Good morning harmonious tranquil singing birds.
Good morning new time and heartening first words.
Good morning body pillow held so tight.
Good morning Dear Love until we say good afternoon.
Good night.

Dear Love,

You my muthafuckin chill
A cool ass attitude
That lead soprano sax
Heart thumping, deep moan love mood.
That bonafide rhythm
From snares, hi-hats, tom's, sticks and a kick
That heart racing 88 keys solo
Damn baby you the shit.
A trumpet yelling at the top of its peak
Hell, you make my soul swoon
Sweat build up
Stomach and knees weak.
Delicious purple grape bite
Drink juices that drip from your lip.
Soul connection, my Heaven
Slip in your hips to take a sip. ...yeah.

Can I tap into you & make you drip?
Nectar sweet and sticky for me to sip
Swimming in your seas
Love let me drown I don't want to come up, let me stay down.
Let me play in your rain and splash around
Swallow you whole.
So wet on my mouth.
Run down my chin.
Again & again.
"Ooh SHIT..." let the battle begin. "
Wait, wait, wait" to "please don't quit"
Somehow now you're on top, lips to lips
Rockin back and forth & circular motions I'm ready to float in your exotic ocean.
You lean back slight, to open up just right
Body start twitching as I take a good bite.
Licking you...."Oh god!"
Then you push me
Can't wait to hear you moan while suckin on your Pus...

Hello Love,

Am I awake or sleeping?
Pillowy fine skin. Wonted scent.
Faint brush from an extremity
I've fallen for you without intent.

Distance & time, I'll linger.
A cocooned caterpillar
A facial caress from a finger.
Natural release and healer.

Darling. Do not appease my adoration
Accept an eternity of my affection.
Do as you please,
Proceed in Heaven's direction.

Unknown peace encountered
Delivered for me to take.
If you are my solitude for to rest
I don't want to wake.

Can I die in your arms and be reborn?
Can I come to you and repair what's torn?
Once complete, there's no need to mourn
Cause we became one in a new form.
Hi Love. Honor and respect from Peace.
Introduce new components of life to greet.
Show me the world. I'll show you wonders.
Show me calm. I'll show you comfort.
Say truthful words. Make time congeal.
A kiss last forever. Life finally feels real.
Nothing about this process is easy
But it's purposeful and has meaning.
Where the world can be deceiving
Love please don't ever leave me.
You're my hope. You're my truth.
God is glorious and you are the proof.

Hi Love. Wit yo sexy ass.
Shorty you bad as fuck.
I hope my cusswords aren't too abrupt
I'm just speaking my mind about that behind
Hips fillin out those jeans.
Shid you fine.
Those long ass legs wrap around nicely
Nice full lips.
Almond eyes entice me.
Long neck, arms and fingers.
Time to explore.
A beautifully constructed sculpture that's hard to ignore.
Yo, I hope you don't mind.
Gimmie a little time.
I want all my shit together before you become mine.
Don't worry about me doe.
Ain't no one a distraction.
You got my full attention.
Love you the main attraction.
The only one that gives me complete satisfaction.
I promise that you're the key to any of my reactions.
Especially if its preparation for sexual interaction
Or if its rhymes to help express my Love & my passion.

I feel like I'm alive for the first time in my life.
It all happened so fast. Suddenly everything was all right.
So broken. I was full darkness and pain.
It wasn't anyone's fault, there was no one to blame.
No pointing fingers, that makes the pain linger.
The new Love in my heart just made me a believer.
I want to live. I want to experience time.
Especially if it's a life where I'm yours and you are mine.

I wish I was the pillow resting your head.

I wish I was the blanket you're wrapped up in.

I wish I was the bed that you're lying on to sleep.

I wish I was the comfort giving you relief.

I want to be the second most important thing you require.

Until we exit in the rapture or time cease and expire.

I want to be the one you come to when you need love and direction.

Keep you covered with acts of service, physical touch & affection.

There are other ways to explore you than taking your panties down while kissing every inch of you slowly. Then licking my way back up which will hopefully have your nerves wrecked as I make a quick stop and have you shaking uncontrollably.

On to the waistline, bellybutton, stomach, breast, collarbone, shoulder, arms, hands, fingers, lips, they all get affection.

There are so many other ways to explore you like intimate talks, taking long walks at a park. I don't know. You make the selection. Either way, I'm down.

Good morning.
Wake up yawning.
God is Great.
Anticipating the day.
Can't wait to see your face.
You're only downstairs.
Got to get myself prepared.
Before I see your presence.
In love with your essence.
A blessing.
Brush my teeth.
Wash my face.
Anxious by the second.
Your body like a weapon.
Face of heavens light.
Hit the steps getting hyped.
Look at you on the couch, relaxed looking right.
Can you be my breakfast?
Just one bite?
Can I have this moment here for the rest of my life?

Pour out til empty. I'll refill your love.
Pour out, don't feel guilty. Let's see what it does.
Pour out. Come with me. Let's pray just because.
Pour out. Yell out joys, frustrations, whatever.
I'm here no matter what it was.
I'll always replenish you during our soul's journey.
Merging beings, intertwined.
Conjoined astronomically through eternity.
Supernatural beings, biblical practice and principals.
Essential manifestations keeping fleshly habits minimal.
There's nothing about our expedition that's typical.
Regular, plain, common, ordinary, traditional.
Creating our own environment instead of following
handed down rituals.
So please pour out.
Give what you need to give. I got you.
Failure isn't an option. I'll do what's necessary to provide.
Love, I don't doubt you.
With support, genuine care and caution.
I promise I won't drop you.
Believe me? It's ok, I'll show you.
Cause I don't want to do this new life without you.

No need to wonder
Winter to summer you the reason.
Something to believe in
With each passing season.
Snowflakes to rainfall
Time helps us evolve
Into something brand new
We bloom from the cocoon.
Watching the full moon
Wondering how soon.
Until I get to keep you Love you.
I beseech you.
Lay in bed beneath you
Alex Isley serenades.
As 'Into Orbit' plays
In your eyes I gaze.
So much I wanna say.
You my night, you my day.
I won't get on your nerves
I'll always keep you encouraged.
I want to earn it all
Be the man that you deserve.
Not just another boy
Charming with kind words.
I'll listen to your concerns
Keep your heart preserved.
I hope you good with me
I'm a regular music loving nerd.

Give me every morning
Give me every afternoon
Give me every night
Of making love to you.

Please pardon me
I'm on my Lionel Ritchie.
It's you I've been lookin for
Bonjour mi amour.
Love is right on time
Woman you look divine.
I hope I match your mood Expectations.
Attitude. Filled with gratitude
That I have you in my life.
Thank you for taking me
I promise to treat you right.
Despite all of the stressin'
It was all God's blessin'.
I accepted every lesson
To be built to your perfection.
Woman, you're the exception
Focus of my affection.
As long as I'm alive
You'll have me for protection.
I'm here no need to fear
Destiny is in our hands.
To love, honor & cherish
The hopes for future plans.
 Travel & romance
Frankincense and Myrrh.
Allow things to walk its course
Let's see what all occurs.
We in different time zones

You don't have to come for me.
I'll come and get you
Miss you. My one and only.

Excited to see your face
Communicate across states
It hard to concentrate
Dreams of you getting ate.
Can't wait to get a taste.
Wrap my arms around your waist.
As I whisper from behind
"Love, will you be mine?"
We skip the wine and dine
Kissin you on your spine
As I slowly lift your shirt
What should we do first?
Unsnapped bra,
No panties
Kiss your lips
Pay homage to your body
I'm caressing every inch
Hearing you say my name
Mixed in with your moans
You saying nasty stuff
Girl you turnin me on.
As we connect bodies, I pick you up
Put you gently on my lap "Sir please wake up...
We've reached our destination
Please exit the plane
Thank you for flying with us
We hope to see you again." ...damn.

Can you? Will you?
Accept me as is.
I hope that you'll take me.
Look pass what I did.
Whatever I've done
Please put it behind as I have.
I don't want to ruin a beautiful future
because of an ugly past.
Can you? Will you? Accept me as is.
I'll gladly take you Love.
No matter what you've hid.
No matter what's happened
that left you bruised
I only want to help you heal
if it's me that you choose.
My Love...

Dear Love.

Thank you for taking care of me.
I'll do all you need to take care of you too.
Kiss you, hug you, serve you, and Love you.
Be honest & loyal. Whatever you need I'll do.
I want to. There's nothing I'd rather get done.
You are the love of my life. Since 96 you've been the one.
No distance will hinder this completely beautiful &
passionate bond.
Let's continue to bloom. My tears of joy can water the
seed of calm.

Printed in Great Britain
by Amazon

38452721R00030